NELSON MATHEMATICS 3
Towards Level 3

PUPILS' BOOK 1

Nelson

Thomas Nelson and Sons Ltd
Nelson House   Mayfield Road
Walton-on-Thames   Surrey
KT12 5PL   UK

Thomas Nelson Australia
102 Dodds Street
South Melbourne
Victoria 3205
Australia

Nelson Canada
1120 Birchmount Road
Scarborough   Ontario
M1K 5G4   Canada

Authors and consultants
New Edition
Bill Domoney
Paul Harrison

First Edition
Bill Domoney
Peter Gash
Lorely James
Ann Sawyer
Owen Tregaskis
Diana Wright

Contributor
Jane Nicholas

Acknowledgements
Photography
Chris Ridgers: page 85 (middle right); Richard and Sally Greenhill: page 85 (top and middle left); Greg Evans: page 85 (bottom).

Design
Julia King, Thumbnail Graphics

Produced by **Ian Foulis & Associates**

New Edition © Thomas Nelson & Sons Ltd 1995
First published by Thomas Nelson & Sons Ltd 1991

ISBN 0-17-421855-9 (single copies)
ISBN 0-17-421857-5 (pack of eight)
NPN 9 8 7 6 5 4 3

All rights reserved. No paragraph of this production may be reproduced, copied or transmitted save with written permission or in accordance with the provisions of the Copyright, Design and Patents Act 1988, or under the terms of any licence permitting limited copying issued by the Copyright Licensing Agency, 90 Tottenham Court Road, London W1P 9HE.

Any person who does any unauthorised act in relation to his publication may be liable to criminal prosecution and civil claims for damages.

Printed in China

CONTENTS

The colour band at the foot of each page indicates the relevant section of the **Teacher's Resource File, Level 3.**

Number

Addition and subtraction to 100
Using a number line to add and subtract 4-5
Using interlocking cubes to solve problems 6-7
Using addition and subtraction squares or tables 30-31
Making number sentences from partitioned sets 32
Completing fact wheels for 11, 12, 13, 14 33
Adding and subtracting numbers up to 20 58
Filling in missing numbers and signs 59

Multiplication
Repeating the addition of 2s or 5s 8-9
Multiplication or repeated addition using equal sets 10-11
Multiplying by 2 34-35
Interpreting equal jumps on a number line as number sentences 36-37
Multiplying by 5 60-61
Multiplying by 3 62-63

Division
Sharing into equal sets of 2 or 4 12-13
Identifying a half or quarter of a set 38-39
Identifying a third, half or quarter of a set 64-65

Money
Repeated addition of coins 14
Using a ready reckoner 15
Counting coins and matching amounts of money 70-71

Number patterns
Varying patterns to predict and investigate the outcome 16-17
Completing number patterns based on tens and hundreds 72
Using patterns in addition 73

Numbers to 1000
Analysing numbers using hundreds, tens and ones equipment 40-41
Interpreting and correcting abacus pictures showing hundreds, tens and ones 42-43
Comparing and ordering numbers 44-45
Translating from pictures and words to numerals 66-67
Comparing three-digit numbers in terms of biggest and smallest 68
Ordering numbers to 1000 69

Shape and Space

3-D shapes
Naming and identifying 3-D shapes 18-19, 74-75

2-D shapes
Identifying 2-D shapes 20-21
Counting sides in 2-D shapes 46
Making and naming 2-D shapes 47
Identifying and naming irregular 2-D shapes 76
Tessellating with irregular 2-D shapes 77

Measures

Length
Measuring with a metre measure 22
Estimating and measuring in metres 23, 48-49
Measuring everyday objects 78
Measuring and drawing lines 79

Weight
Estimating and weighing in kilograms 24-25
Reading scales and solving problems in kilograms 50-51

Capacity
Comparing and measuring capacities in litres 26-27
Making comparisons using non-standard and litre measures 52-53

Time
Estimating and timing activities in seconds, minutes, hours 54-55
Making a timer and timing to the nearest second 80
Reading times from stopwatches and comparing them 81

Area
Comparing areas to one square metre 82
Measuring area by counting squares 83

Handling Data

Handling data
Interpreting a block graph or bar chart 28-29
Drawing and interpreting a bar chart 56-57
Interpreting and drawing pictograms 84-85

Glossary 86-88

Number line sums

For each of these sums draw a number line from 0 to 20.
Find the starting number.
To add, count on:

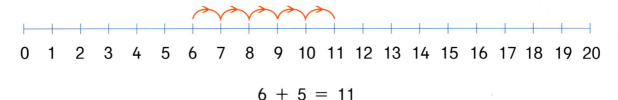

$6 + 5 = 11$

To subtract, count back:

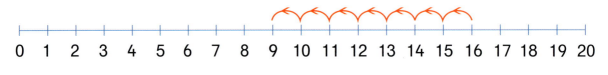

$16 - 7 = 9$

Show the jumps on your number lines and write the answers.

1. $9 + 8 = $ ___
2. $14 - 8 = $ ___
3. $6 + 13 = $ ___
4. $9 + 9 = $ ___
5. $12 - 1 = $ ___
6. $14 + 5 = $ ___

Write the sums that these number lines show.

● shows the starting number

7.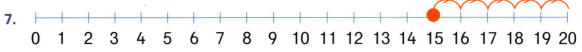

8.

9.

Bus sums

Use this number line to help you.

0 1 2 3 4 5 6 7 8 9 10 11 12 13 14 15 16 17 18 19 20

1. Which buses belong in garage 11?
2. Which buses belong in garage 13?
3. Which buses belong in garage 15?

Make up a sum whose answer is:

4. 9
5. 16
6. 19

Rod sums

> You will need interlocking cubes.

Make this rod.

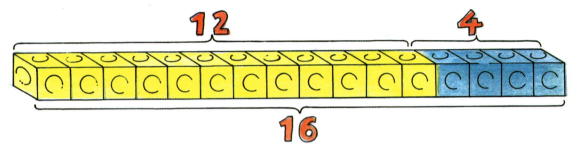

The rod shows these four sums:

    12 + 4 = 16   4 + 12 = 16   16 − 12 = 4   16 − 4 = 12

Make these rods. Write the four sums that each one shows.

1.

2.

3.

4.

5.

Adding and subtracting problems

> You will need interlocking cubes.

Use interlocking cubes to help you.
Write the missing numbers.

1. ☐ + 6 = 13
2. ☐ + 9 = 15
3. ☐ + 4 = 12
4. 5 + ☐ = 14
5. 3 + ☐ = 11
6. 8 + ☐ = 17

Write the answers to these problems.

7. A football team needs 11 players. It has only 4. How many more players are needed?

8. Ranjit has 5 marbles. He won another 8. How many does he have now?

9. Sammy planted 15 seeds. Only 8 came up. How many did not grow?

10. Sally scored 16 points. Ricky scored 9. What is the difference?

11. There were 18 cartons of milk in the class. 9 children took one each. How many were left?

12. Simran needs 8 more stamps to make 14 altogether. How many does she have already?

> There is more about adding and subtracting on page 30.

Twos all around

2 + 2 + 2 + 2 + 2 + 2 = 12

There are 12 legs under these dresses.

Write the adding sum for each of these pictures.

1. How many wheels? 2. How many wings?

3. How many eyes?

4. How many ears?

5. How many legs?

6. How many shoes are there in your class today?
   Write down all the twos and count them. Add them all up.

7. Make a list of all the things you know that come in twos.

Multiplication   Unit 1   Repeated addition of 2

Counting toes

Each of your feet has 5 toes.

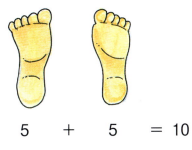

5 + 5 = 10

10 toes altogether

How many toes inside these socks and shoes? Write each sum.

7. How many toes in your group today? Draw the feet. Write down the sum.

Counting sets

2 sets.

5 apples in each set.

There are 10 apples altogether.

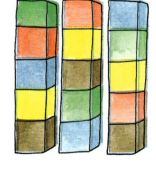

1. How many sets?

2. How many cubes in each set?

3. How many cubes altogether?

4. How many sets?

5. How many children in each set?

6. How many children altogether?

7. How many sets?

8. How many eggs in each set?

9. How many eggs altogether?

10. Draw 3 sets of 4 sweets. How many sweets altogether?

11. Draw 5 sets of 3 sweets. How many sweets altogether?

Multiplication   Unit 2   Multiplication using sets

Flower sets

4 sets of 2 make 8. 2 + 2 + 2 + 2 = 8

Copy the pictures.

Copy the sums and fill in the missing numbers.

1.

   sets of ☐ make ☐   3 + 3 + 3 + 3 + 3 + 3 + 3 = ☐

2.

   ☐ sets of ☐ make ☐   4 + 4 + 4 + 4 = ☐

3.    4.

   ☐ sets of ☐ make ☐   ☐ sets of ☐ make ☐
   1 + 1 + 1 + 1 = ☐   5 + 5 = ☐

Draw these sets of flowers.

Write the adding sum underneath.

5. 3 sets of 5.   6. 4 sets of 2.

 There is more about adding sets on page 34.

Multiplication   Unit 2   Adding equal sets   11

Sharing between two

6 sweets are shared equally between 2 children. Each gets 3 sweets.

Share these things equally.

1. How many sweets?
2. How many children?
3. How many sweets each?

4. How many cakes?
5. How many children?
6. How many cakes each?

7. How many apples?
8. How many children?
9. How many apples each?

10. How many pennies?
11. How many children?
12. How many pennies each?

Division   Unit 1   Equal sharing into 2 sets

Sharing between four

8 bones are shared equally between 4 dogs. Each gets 2 bones.

Share these things equally.

1. How many nuts?
2. How many squirrels?
3. How many nuts each?

4. How many leaves?
5. How many rabbits?
6. How many leaves each?

7. How many worms?
8. How many birds?
9. How many worms each?

10. How many flies?
11. How many spiders?
12. How many flies each?

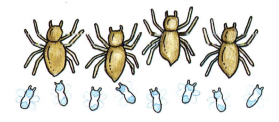

There is more about sharing on page 38.

Money problems

> You will need 2p, 5p, 10p, 20p and 50p coins.

Answer these problems. Use coins to help you.

1. Jane has 6 stickers.
   Each sticker cost 10p.
   How much did they cost altogether?

2. Dexter has 30 pencils.
   Each pencil cost 10p.
   How much did they cost altogether?

3. Peter has 9 cars.
   Each car cost 50p.
   How much did they cost altogether?

4. Tracy has 24 sweets.
   Each sweet cost 2p.
   How much did they cost altogether?

5. Gemma has 4 hair bobbles. Each bobble cost 20p.
   How much did they cost altogether?

6. Kar Wei has 20 marbles. Each marble cost 15p.
   How much did they cost altogether?

Ready reckoner

If 1 stamp costs 15p
3 stamps cost 45p.

	2p	5p	8p	15p	20p
1	2p	5p	8p	15p	20p
2	4p	10p	16p	30p	40p
3	6p	15p	24p	45p	60p
4	8p	20p	32p	60p	80p
5	10p	25p	40p	75p	£1.00

Use the ready reckoner to help you find the answers to these:

1. If one stamp costs 5p, how much will 4 stamps cost?

2. If one stamp costs 20p, how much will 6 stamps cost?

3. If you have 75p, do you have enough money to buy 5 15p stamps?

4. If one stamp costs 8p, how much will 4 stamps cost?

5. How many 2p stamps can you buy with 15p?

6. How many 15p stamps can you buy with 80p?

7. How many 8p stamps can you buy with 40p?

8. How many 20p stamps can you buy with 90p?

Make up some problems for your friends to try.

There is more about money on page 70.

Money   Unit 1   Using a ready reckoner

Pattern prediction

> You will need isometric and squared paper.

Can you predict the answers?
Use the pattern, 1 green circle, 2 yellow circles.

1. What is the colour of the 18th circle?
2. What is the colour of the 29th circle?

Use the pattern, 2 green circles, 1 yellow circle, 1 white circle.

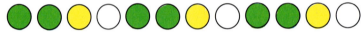

3. What is the colour of the 17th circle?
4. What is the colour of the 34th circle?

Look at this pattern.

5. What is the colour of the 20th circle?
6. What is the colour of the 30th circle?

Copy the patterns onto isometric or squared paper.

Can you extend the patterns?
Will the shapes be the same?

7.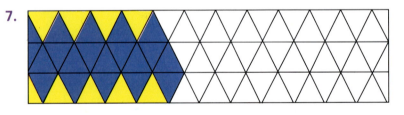

8.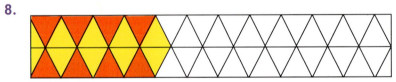

9.

16   Number patterns   Unit 1   Predicting the outcome of extending patterns

Investigating patterns

> You will need squared paper.

Copy and continue these patterns.

1.

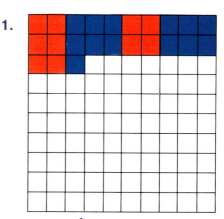

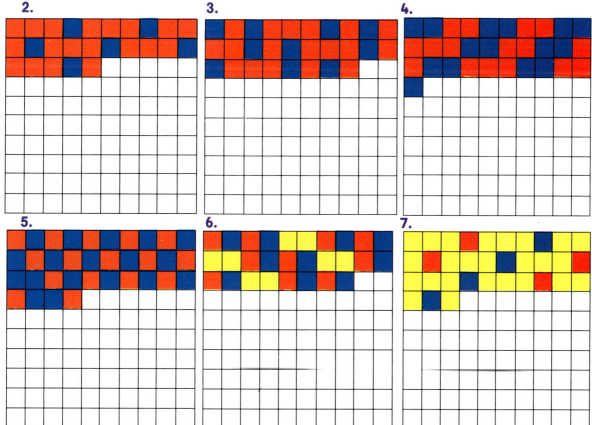

How about changing the size of the grids?
Try 5 x 5, 6 x 6, 8 x 8 or larger.
Does anything happen to the patterns?

> There is more about number patterns on page 72.

What's the name?

Look at these shapes and their names.

Write the names of these shapes.

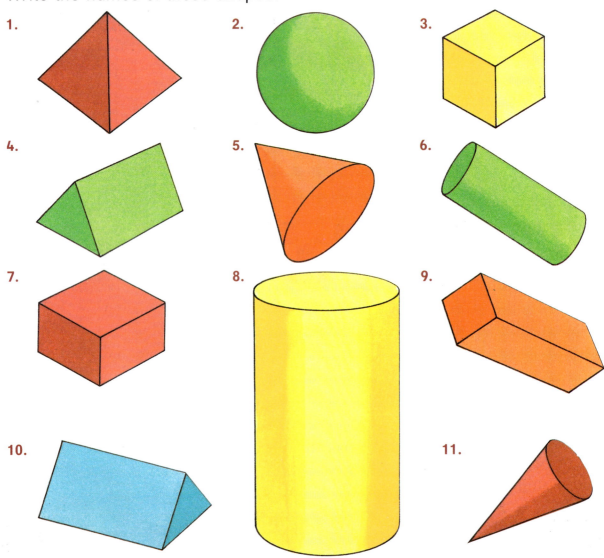

Solid shapes

Here are the names of the solid shapes.

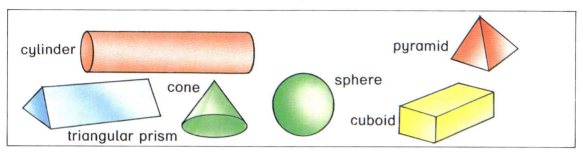

A tin of beans is a cylinder

What shapes are these like?

10. Find some things around the classroom and write down the names of their shapes.

There is more about 3-D shapes on page 74.

Shapes in a church

Look at the drawing of the church.

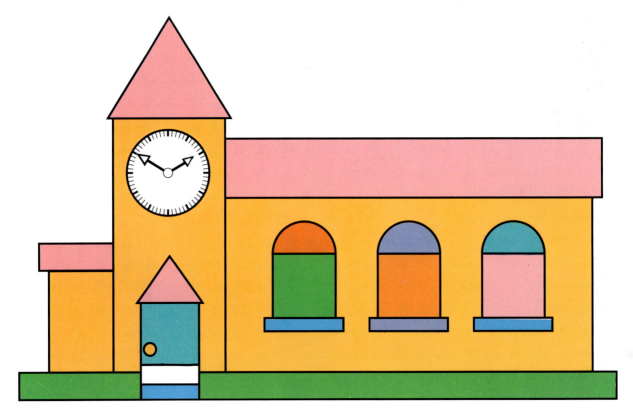

1. How many triangles can you see?

2. How many squares can you see?

3. How many rectangles can you see?

4. How many circles can you see?

5. How many semi-circles can you see?

6. Now draw your own picture using all of these shapes.
   Write down how many of each shape there are in your picture.

Door shapes

Write how many circles, semi-circles, triangles, squares and rectangles you can find in each door.

1.
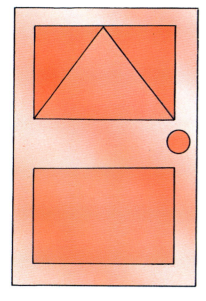

2.
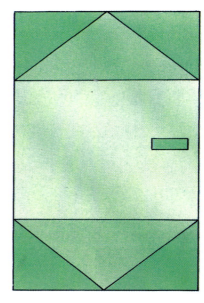

3.
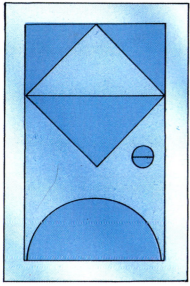

4.
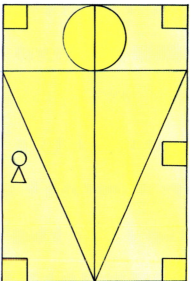

5. Draw your own door and write down how many of each shape you have used.

There is more about 2-D shapes on page 46.

Metre measures

You will need a metre stick, a metre tape or a piece of string 1 metre long.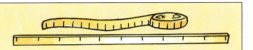

Use your metre stick, tape or string to measure these things.

Find out whether they are about 1 metre, shorter than 1 metre or longer than 1 metre.

1. rug
2. arm span
3. shoe
4. blackboard
5. Think of 2 more things to measure.

Make a chart like this to show your answers.
Put a tick in the right box for each one.

	about 1 metre	shorter than 1 metre	longer than 1 metre
1. rug			
2. arm span			
3. shoe			
4. blackboard			
5.			

Estimating in metres

> You will need a metre stick, a metre tape or a piece of string 1 metre long.

Estimate how many metres each object measures.

Then measure it with a metre stick, tape or string.

1. skipping rope
2. display board
3. wall

 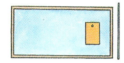 

4. door
5. Think of 2 more objects to estimate and measure.

Make a chart like this for your answers.

Write the number of metres in each box.

	Estimate	Measure
1. skipping rope	metres	metres
2. display board	metres	metres
3. wall	metres	metres
4. door	metres	metres
5.	metres	metres

There is more about measuring length on page 48.

Length   Unit 1   Estimating in metres

Feeling the weight

> You will need a kilogram weight and some objects to weigh.

Choose one of these:

      bag of sugar   a shoe   a book

Hold the object in one hand.
Hold a kilogram weight in the other hand.
Does the object feel less than a kilogram?
    or about the same as a kilogram?
    or more than a kilogram?

Do the same with the other two objects.

Make a chart like this.
Put a tick in the right box for each object.

	less than one kilogram	about one kilogram	more than one kilogram
1. bag of sugar			
2. a shoe			
3. a book			
4.			

Choose some more objects and feel the weight of each.
Put them in your chart.

Weighing in kilograms

You will need a balance, some kilogram weights, and some objects to weigh.

bag of apples

a stone

Plasticine

lunch box

Estimate how many kilograms each object weighs.

Then weigh each object using a balance and kilogram weights.

Make a chart like this for your answers.

Write the number of kilograms in each box.

	Estimate	Actual weight
bag of apples	kg	kg
a stone	kg	kg
Plasticine	kg	kg
lunch box	kg	kg

Find some more objects to weigh. Write them in your chart.

There is more about weighing on page 50.

Weight   Unit 1   Estimating and weighing in kilograms

Looking at litres

You will need a litre measure.

Collect some different containers like these.

Estimate whether each one holds less than a litre, more than a litre, or about one litre.

Then find out by pouring from your litre measure.

Make a chart like this.

Write the name of the container in the right column.

less than 1 litre	about 1 litre	more than 1 litre

How many litres?

> You will need a litre measure.

Find some large containers that you could measure in litres.

For each container:

estimate how many litres it holds;
use water or sand and a litre container to find out the actual number of litres each container holds; then find out the difference between your estimate and the actual number.

Make a chart like this:

Container	I estimate it holds	It actually holds	Difference
	litres	litres	litres
	litres	litres	litres
	litres	litres	litres

> There is more about litres on page 52.

Capacity   Unit 1   Measuring in litres

Pet graph

Here is a block graph.

It shows the pets owned by children in a class.

1. How many cats are there?
2. How many dogs are there?
3. Which pet do 3 children each own?
4. Which pet do 2 children each own?
5. How many hamsters are there?
6. Which pet do 6 children each own?
7. How many pets are there altogether?
8. What is the most popular pet?
9. Now make your own block graph to show which pets are owned by children in your class.

Handling data   Unit 1   Interpreting a block graph

Birthday bar chart

We drew this bar chart to show the birthday months of everyone in our class.

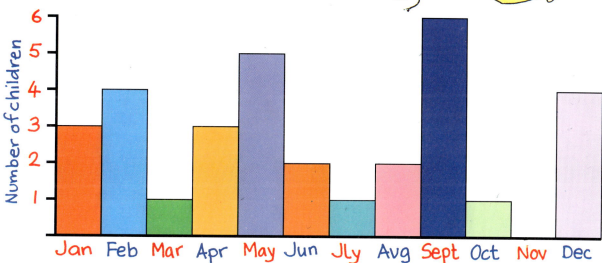

Write the missing words and numbers.

1. There are no birthdays in _____.
2. Most birthdays are in _____.
3. There are ___ birthdays in May.
4. In _____ and _____ there are 2 birthdays.

There are 3 months with the same number of birthdays.

5. They are _____, _____ and _____.
6. There are ___ children in this class.
7. Now make your own birthday bar chart for your class. Write some questions about the chart.

There is more about graphs on page 56.

Handling data   Unit 1   Interpreting a bar chart

Adding square

You can use this square to add two numbers.

6 + 9
find one number along here

find the other number along here

+	0	1	2	3	4	5	6	7	8	9	10
0	0	1	2	3	4	5	6	7	8	9	10
1	1	2	3	4	5	6	7	8	9	10	11
2	2	3	4	5	6	7	8	9	10	11	12
3	3	4	5	6	7	8	9	10	11	12	13
4	4	5	6	7	8	9	10	11	12	13	14
5	5	6	7	8	9	10	11	12	13	14	15
6	6	7	8	9	10	11	12	13	14	15	16
7	7	8	9	10	11	12	13	14	15	16	17
8	8	9	10	11	12	13	14	15	16	17	18
9	9	10	11	12	13	14	15	16	17	18	19
10	10	11	12	13	14	15	16	17	18	19	20

The answer is where the 2 numbers meet

6 + 9 = 15

Use the square to answer these:

1. 4 + 5 =   **2.** 7 + 8 =   **3.** 9 + 9 =
4. 8 + 0 =   **5.** 4 + 8 =   **6.** 4 + 2 =
7. Find a 16 in the square. What two numbers meet there?
8. Complete this sum: ☐ + ☐ = 16
9. Find other 16s. Write their sums.

Find these numbers. Write their sums.

10. 20   **11.** 19   **12.** 18

Addition and subtraction to 100   Unit 3   Using an addition square

Adding and subtracting puzzles

Can you see how this subtracting puzzle is being done?

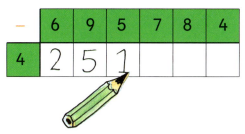

Copy these adding and subtracting puzzles.

Fill in the empty squares.

Be careful! Look at the sign.

1.

+	0	1	2	3	4	5	6	7	8	9
6										

2.

−	5	9	7	8	6	4
3						

3.

+	2	4	6	1	3	5
4						

4.

−	8	3	4	10	9	2	6	5	7
2									

Now try these.

5.

+	3	4	5
3			
4			
5			

6.

−	7	10	9
5			
6			
3			

7.

+	4	5	6
7			
8			
9			

Addition and subtraction to 100   Unit 3   Addition and subtraction tables practice

Ladybird numbers

The spots on this ladybird show:

2 + 9 = 11   9 + 2 = 11
11 − 2 = 9   11 − 9 = 2

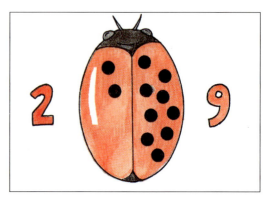

Write the four number sentences that these ladybirds show:

1.

2.

3.

4.

5.

6.

7. Draw 2 different ladybirds with 12 spots.
   Write the number sentences for each one.

Fact wheels

In a fact wheel the two outside numbers add up to the number in the middle.

There are some letters instead of numbers in these fact wheels.

Write the number that each letter stands for.

1.

2.

3.

4.

There is more about number facts on page 58.

How many twos?

This picture shows
2 + 2 + 2 = 6
3 twos make 6
3 x 2 = 6

Write in three ways what these pictures show.

1.

2.

3.

4.

5.

Draw pictures to show these. Then write the answer.

6. 6 x 2

7. 9 x 2

Problems with twos

There are 2 cars in a box.

How many cars in 4 boxes?

4 × 2 = 8. So in 4 boxes there are 8 cars.

Read the problem. Write the sum. Write the answer.

1. There are 2 balls in a bag. How many balls in 3 bags?

2. There are 2 chocolates in a packet. How many in 5 packets?

3. There are 2 shoes in a box. How many shoes in 2 boxes?

4. There are 2 glasses in a set. How many in 7 sets?

5. There are 2 sticks of rock in a packet. How many in 10 packets?

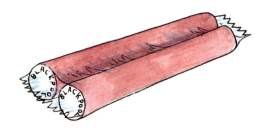

6. One cake costs 2p. How much do 8 cakes cost?

Multiplication   Unit 3   Problems involving multiplication by 2

Jumping in twos

This picture shows
4 jumps of 2 make 8
2 + 2 + 2 + 2 = 8
4 x 2 = 8

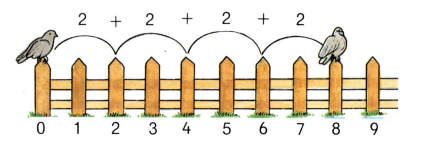

Write in three ways what these pictures show.

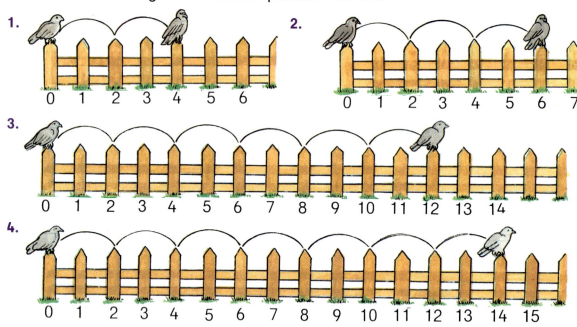

Write in three ways what these number lines show.

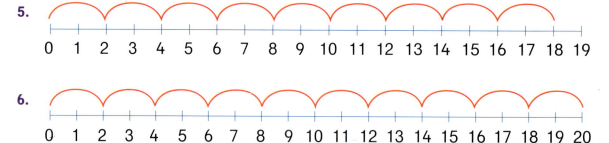

Draw number lines to show these. Write the answers.

7. 4 x 2

8. 8 x 2

More equal jumps

This number line shows 4 jumps of 3 make 12

3 + 3 + 3 + 3 = 12   4 x 3 = 12

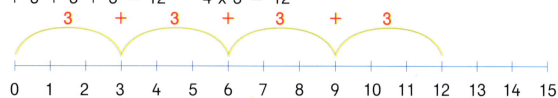

Write in three ways what these number lines show:

1.

2.

3.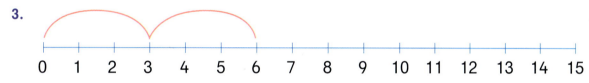

4.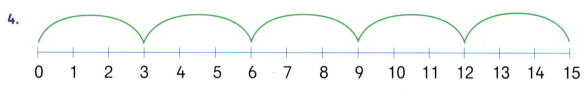

5.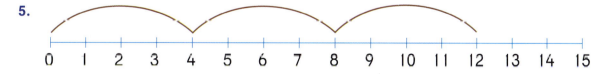

For each of these draw a number line.
Show the jumps. Write the answer.

6. 6 jumps of 2   7. 2 jumps of 4   8. 4 x 2

 There is more about multiplying on page 60.

Finding half

> You will need counters and a small stick or piece of string.

half half

This set of 6 counters has been cut into <u>two</u> equal parts.

Each part is called a <u>half</u>. A <u>half</u> of 6 is 3.

Use a small stick or piece of string to cut these sets into two equal parts.

Finish the sentences.

1.

   A half of 4 is ___.

2.

   A half of 2 is ___.

3.

   A half of 8 is ___.

4.

   A half of 10 is ___.

5.

   A half of 12 is ___.

Showing a quarter

You will need small sticks or pieces of string and counters.

quarter   quarter   quarter   quarter

This set of 8 ladybirds has been cut into <u>four</u> equal parts.

Each part is called a quarter. A quarter of 8 is 2.

Use small sticks or pieces of string to cut these sets into four equal parts. You could use the counters to help you.

Finish the sentences.

1.

   A quarter of 4 is ___.

2.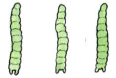

   A quarter of 12 is ___.

3.

   A quarter of 16 is ___.

4.

   A quarter of 20 is ___.

 There is more about cutting into equal parts on page 64.

Division   Unit 2   Identifying a quarter of a set

Hundreds, tens and ones

This picture shows:

1 hundred 5 tens 6 ones

Write how many hundreds, tens and ones these pictures show.

1.

2.

3.

4.

5.

6.

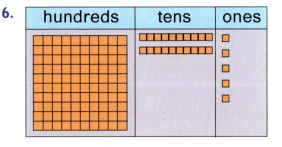

40   Numbers to 1000   Unit 1   Analysing numbers

More hundreds, tens and ones

This picture shows
1 <u>hundred</u> 2 <u>tens</u> 1 <u>one</u>.
The number is 121.

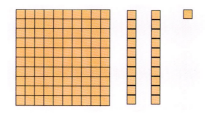

Write how many hundreds, tens and ones these pictures show.
Then write the number.

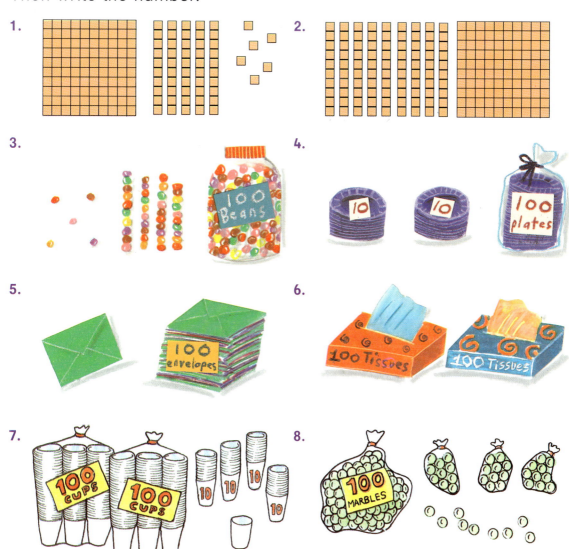

Numbers to 1000   Unit 1   Interpreting pictures of hundreds, tens and ones

Abacus numbers

The number this abacus shows is 122.

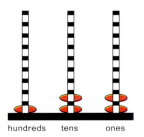

Write the numbers these abacuses show:

1.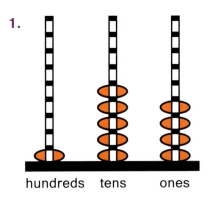
2.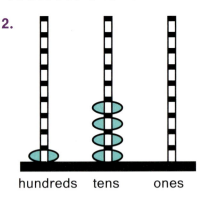
3.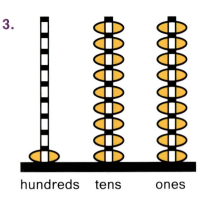
4.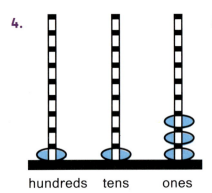
5.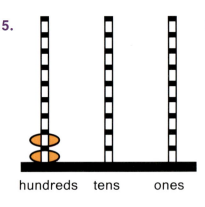
6.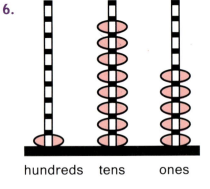
7.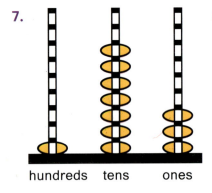
8.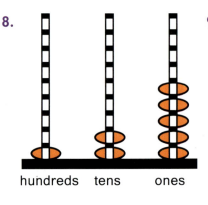
9.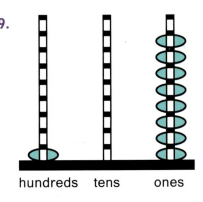

Abacus mistakes

Copy these abacuses and numbers.
Beware! There are lots of mistakes!
Draw more beads or write in extra hundreds, tens or ones numbers to make them right.

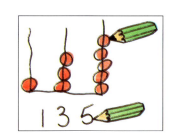

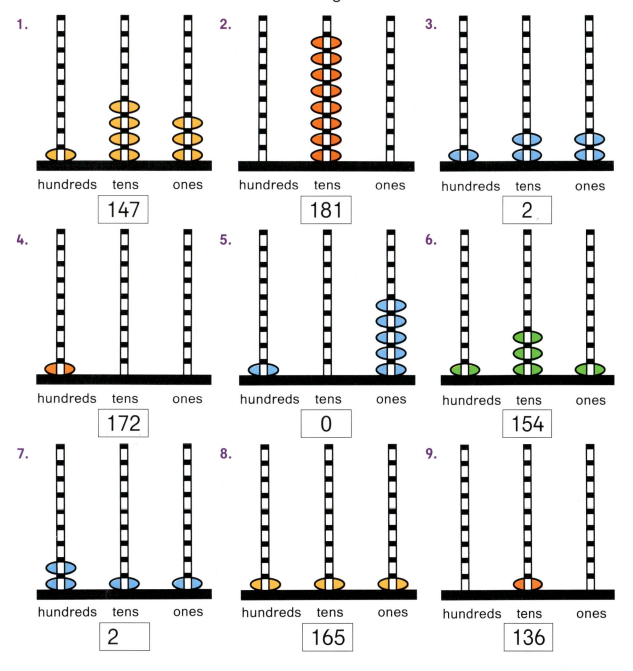

Numbers to 1000   Unit 2   Correcting abacus pictures and numbers

43

Fairground fun

The children have been playing darts at the fair.

1. Who won a teddy?
2. Who won a toy car?
3. Who won a lolly?
4. Who had the smallest score?
5. Who had the biggest score?
6. Put their scores in order from the smallest to the biggest.

Copy these numbers. Put > or < between them.

> means "is bigger than"	< means "is smaller than"
50 > 20	11 < 93

7. 37   73
8. 54   45
9. 98   89
10. 67   76
11. 93   39
12. 44   74

44   Numbers to 1000   Unit 3   Comparing and ordering numbers to 100

From smallest to biggest

	90	21	72	50	170	129	100	5
	5	21	50	72	90	100	129	170

Write these numbers again, putting them in order, with the smallest number first and the biggest number last.

1.   121   9   89   11   26   48   62   163

2.   75   25   4   133   21   165   39   86

3.   111   21   32   144   94   33   57   3

4.   162   17   63   29   35   82   51   21

5.   14   52   21   37   145   92   135   42

6.   99   36   8   47   61   125   22   173

There is more about putting numbers in order on page 68.

Numbers to 1000   Unit 3   Ordering numbers to 200

Count the sides

Look at the shapes below.
Count the number of sides on each shape.

How many shapes have:

1. 3 sides?   2. 4 sides?   3. 5 sides?   4. 6 sides?

Draw a shape with:

5. 3 sides   6. 4 sides   7. 5 sides   8. 6 sides.

Geostrip shapes

You will need Geostrips and paper fasteners.

Karina used four Geostrips and four paper-fasteners to make these shapes.

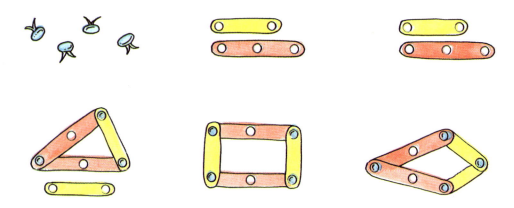

Make two shapes with each of these sets of Geostrips.

Draw each shape. Write the name if you know it.

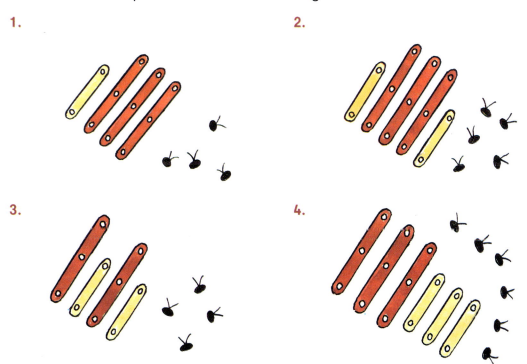

2-D shapes   Unit 2   *Making regular and irregular 2-D shapes with a fixed number of sides*

How well can you estimate?

> You will need a metre stick.

1. Choose some distances around the school.
   First, estimate how far they are in metres.
   Then measure them.
   Work out the difference between your estimate and the answer.

   Write your answers in a chart like this.

Distance	My guess	Measure	Difference
From my seat to the door	10 metres	7½ metres	2½ metres

2. Use your steps to help work out distances.

   start   finish

   Put a marker on the floor. Use a pencil or rubber.
   Walk 5 steps. Put another marker on the floor.
   Look at the distance between the two markers.
   Estimate how many metres you walked and write it down.
   Now measure the distance between the two markers.
   Was your estimate close?

   Do the same test for:

   10 steps   15 steps   20 steps

   Is there a pattern? How many steps do you need to go 3 m?
   Check your estimate.

How long and how high?

Make a sensible guess. Write down the answers.

1.
Is a bike:
about 2 m long?
about 20 m long?
about 200 m long?

2.
Is a lamp post:
about 6 m high?
about 60 m high?
about 600 m high?

3.
Is a house:
about 1 m high?
about 10 m high?
about 100 m high?

4.
Is a train:
about 2 m long?
about 20 m long?
about 200 m long?

5.
Is a car:
about 3 m long?
about 30 m long?
about 300 m long?

6.
Is an oak tree:
about 4 m high?
about 40 m high?
about 400 m high?

7.
Is a fireman's ladder:
about 1 m long?
about 10 m long?
about 100 m long?

8.
Is an elephant:
about 3 m high?
about 30 m high?
about 300 m high?

9.
Is a running track:
about 4 m long?
about 40 m long?
about 400 m long?

You can check some of your estimates by measuring, or looking up the answers in an encyclopedia or *The Guinness Book of Records*. Make up some questions of your own to ask a friend.

There is more about measuring length on page 78.

Length   Unit 2   Making sensible estimates

At the greengrocer's

How much do each of these weigh, to the nearest kilogram?

1.
2.
3.
4.
5.
6.

How much would your bag weigh if you bought:

7. the bananas, potatoes and carrots

8. the apples, pears and potatoes

9. the cabbages, apples and bananas

10. everything?

11. Now make your own shopping list. Write down how much your bag would weigh if you bought the items on the list.

Weight   Unit 2   Reading scales and adding weight in kilograms

Some weighty problems

> You will need personal scales.

Julie needs to take all of these boxes out to her van.
The most she can carry safely in one trip to the van is 40 kg.
This means she can carry the 20 kg box, 15 kg and 5 kg boxes in one trip.
She has worked out she needs five more trips.

1. Write down the weights of the boxes she takes each time.

   Do you know how much **you** weigh?
2. Weigh yourself to the nearest kilogram.
3. Weigh a friend and find the difference in your weights.
4. How much do you both weigh together?
5. Weigh some more friends. Write their names and their weights.

Weight   Unit 2   Solving problems using kilograms.

Litres and cupfuls

> You will need a litre measure and a cup.

Naomi wants to measure how much things hold more accurately than just in litres.

She uses a 1 litre measure and a cup.

For a small container she finds out how many cupfuls it holds.

The vase holds 5 cupfuls

For a large container, first she pours in as many litres as it will hold.

Then she fills up the rest with cupfuls.

She writes how many litres and cupfuls it holds.

The bowl holds 4 litres and 6 cupfuls

Find some containers, big and small.

Use your cup and litre measure to find out how much they hold.

Write the names of the containers and how many cupfuls or how many litres and cupfuls they hold.

Make your own cupfuls measure

> You will need a clear plastic litre bottle, a long paper strip, a pouring funnel and a cup.

Pour one full cup of water into the litre bottle.

Pour in another cupful.

Glue the paper strip to the bottle. Draw a line at the water level. Write 1 by the line.

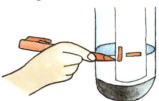

Draw a line where the water level is now. Write 2 by the line.

Keep pouring in full cups of water and drawing lines and numbers until you get near to the top.

This bottle is now your "cupfuls" measure.

You can use your "cupfuls" litre bottle to find out how many cupfuls different containers hold.

If you think a container holds more than a litre you can first pour into a litre measure and then into your "cupfuls" measure.

Find 5 containers. Find out how much they hold in cupfuls or litres and cupfuls. Write down your results.

Capacity   Unit 2   Graduating a container in non-standard units and using it to measure capacity

How long will it take?

> You will need a stopwatch or clock.

Work with a friend.

Make a chart like this:

Activity	less than 1 min	1 min to 5 mins	5 mins to 15 mins	more than 15 mins
1.				
2.				
3.				
4.				

Look at the pictures below.

<u>Estimate</u> how long you think each activity would take.

Write the activity and put a ✔ in the chart to show your estimate.

Then one of you do the activity while the other times it.

Put a ✔ to show the actual time.

1. Put on a coat.

2. Bounce a ball 20 times.

3. Walk around the playground 5 times.

4. Count up to 100.

5. Do a jig-saw puzzle.

6. Copy 50 words from a book.

7. Think of 2 more activities that you could estimate and time.

Sensible times

Look at the activities. How long do you think each one would take?
Choose the best estimate.

1. Eating a meal.

   30 seconds
   5 minutes
   30 minutes
   5 hours

2. Reading 2 pages of a story book.

   10 seconds
   10 minutes
   50 minutes
   10 hours

3. Drinking a glass of water.

   15 seconds
   10 minutes
   15 minutes
   15 hours

4. Having a bath.

   5 seconds
   50 seconds
   20 minutes
   3 hours

5. Opening a parcel.

   1 second
   30 seconds
   30 minutes
   30 hours

6. Changing for P. E.

   5 seconds
   15 seconds
   5 minutes
   5 hours

> There is more about timing on page 80.

Time   Unit 1   Estimating times in seconds, minutes or hours

Sandwich survey

You will need squared paper.

Katie asked everyone in her class what they liked in their sandwiches. She has just started to show the results.

1. Copy Katie's tally chart and write in the missing numbers.
2. Copy Katie's bar chart and finish it for her.

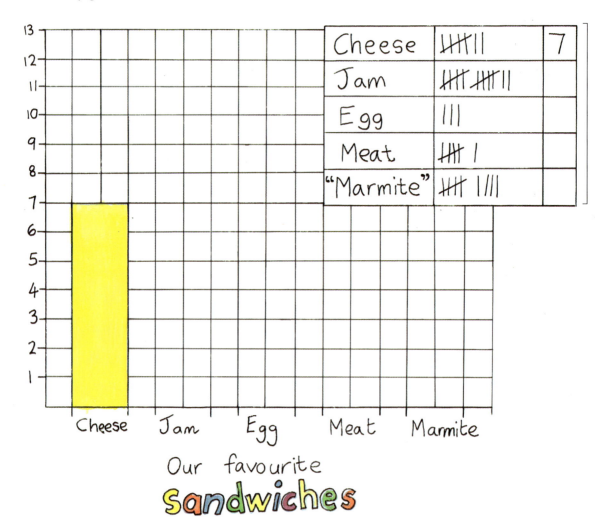

Now find out which sandwiches your class likes.

Make a tally chart and draw a bar chart to show the results.

Sport survey

Here is a bar chart. It was drawn to show the favourite sports of children in a class.

1. What is the most popular sport?
2. How many children liked swimming best?
3. How many children liked gymnastics?
4. What was the third most popular sport?
5. How many children liked rounders?
6. How many more children liked football better than netball?

What do the children in your class like to do in their spare time?

7. Make your own bar chart.

 There is more about graphs on page 84.

Calculator challenge

Pressing the keys changes the display.

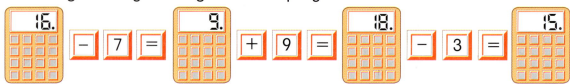

Write the missing display numbers.

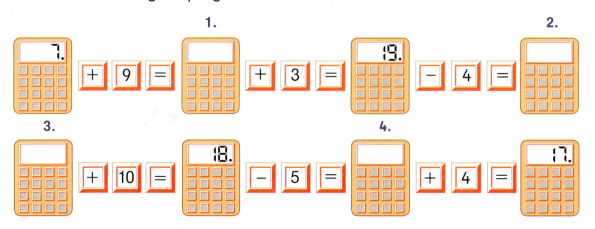

Write the missing key numbers.

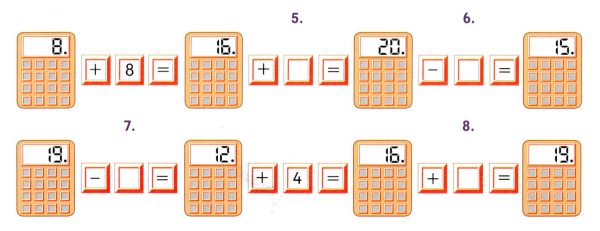

Write the missing key and display numbers.

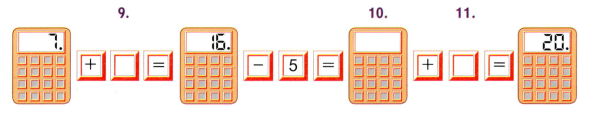

Spilt paint

Oh no! Someone has spilt paint on Pete's work.
Copy each sum and write in the missing numbers and signs.

1. $9 + 9 = \square$

2. $17 \square 9 = 8$

3. $\square + 8 = 17$

4. $11 \square 8 = 19$

5. $18 - 8 = \square$

6. $17 - \square = 11$

7. $8 + \square = 20$

8. $13 + 6 = \square$

9. $18 \square = 14$

10. $17 \square = 20$

11. $16 + 3 \square 9$

12. $19 \square = 9$

Addition and subtraction to 100   Unit 5   Filling in missing numbers and signs

Groups of five

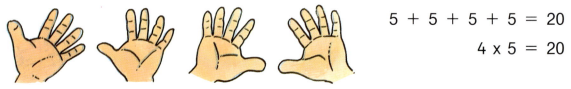

$5 + 5 + 5 + 5 = 20$

$4 \times 5 = 20$

Write an addition sentence and a multiplication sentence for each of these pictures.

1.
2.
3.
4.
5.

Multiplication pictures

The pictures can help you answer the questions.

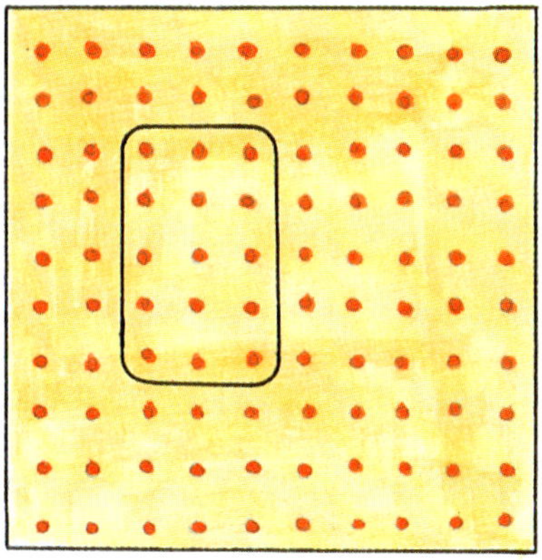

1. 3 x 5 =

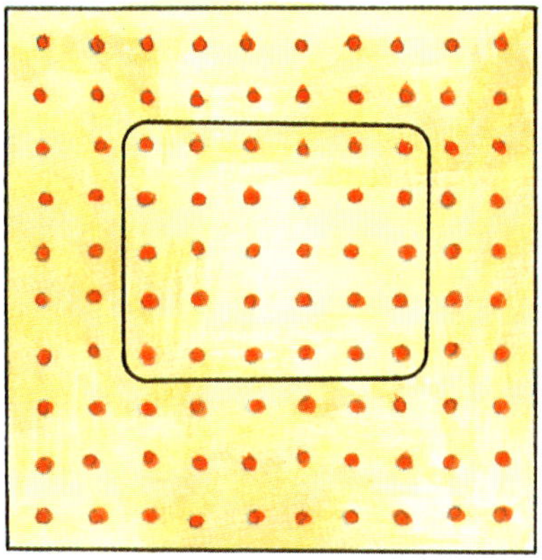

2. 6 x 5 =

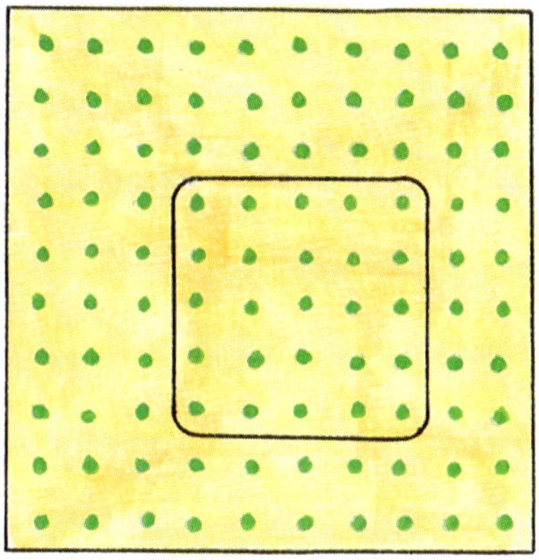

3. 5 x 5 =

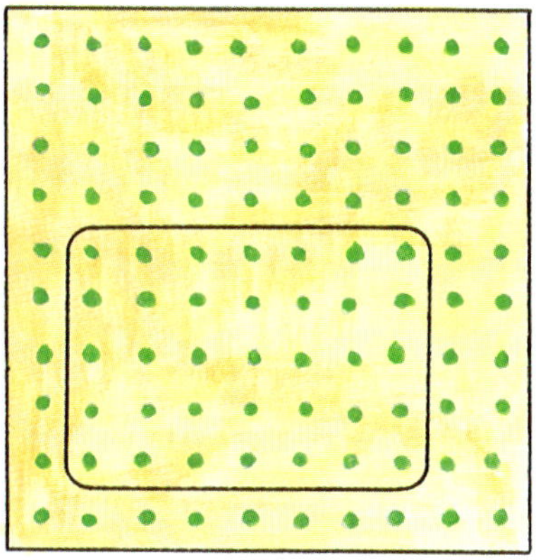

4. 7 x 5 =

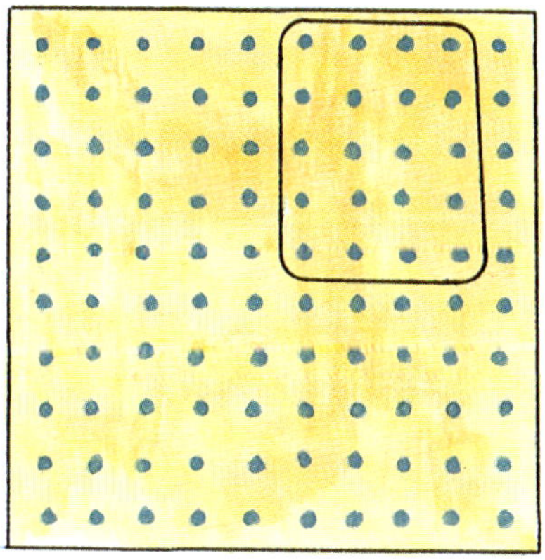

5. 4 x 5 =

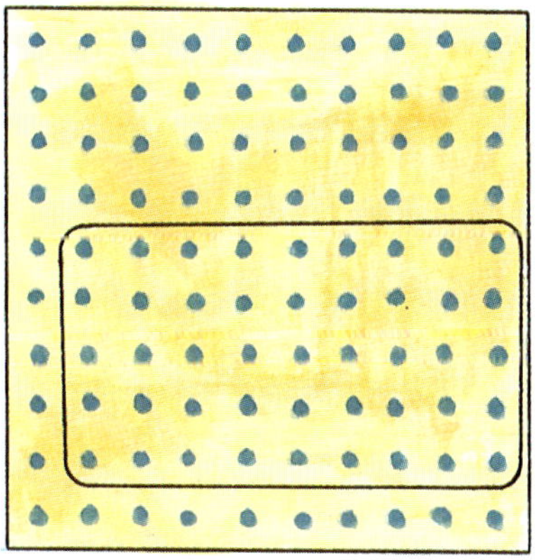

6. 9 x 5 =

Adding and multiplying

3 + 3 + 3 + 3 + 3 = 15

5 x 3 = 15

Write an addition sentence and a multiplication sentence for these pictures.

1.
2.
3.
4.
5.

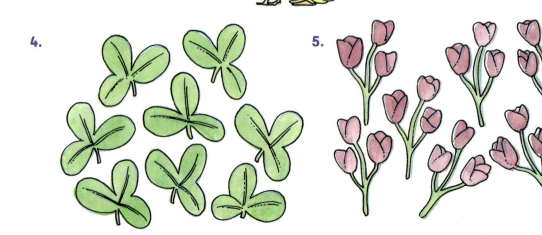

Multiplication   Unit 6   Interpreting sets of 3 as addition and multiplication sentences

Cross numbers

If 5 sticks are laid on top of 3 sticks they cross in 15 places.

5 x 3 = 15

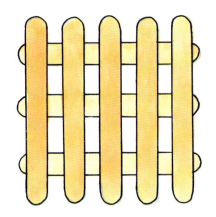

The pictures can help you answer the questions.

1.
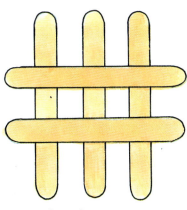

2 x 3 =

2.
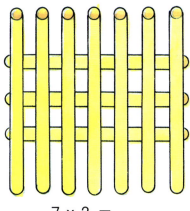

7 x 3 =

3.
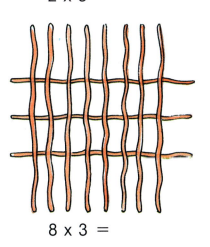

8 x 3 =

4.
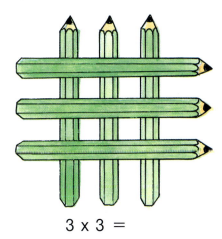

3 x 3 =

You can draw your own pictures for these.

5. 4 x 3 =

6. 6 x 3 =

Multiplication   Unit 6   Multiplying by 3 using arrays

Showing thirds

You will need small sticks or pieces of string and counters.

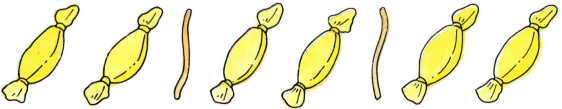

This set of 6 sweets has been cut into <u>three</u> equal parts.

Each part is called a <u>third</u>.

A <u>third</u> of 6 is 2.

Use small sticks or pieces of string to cut these sets into three equal parts. You could use counters to help you.

Copy and finish the sentences.

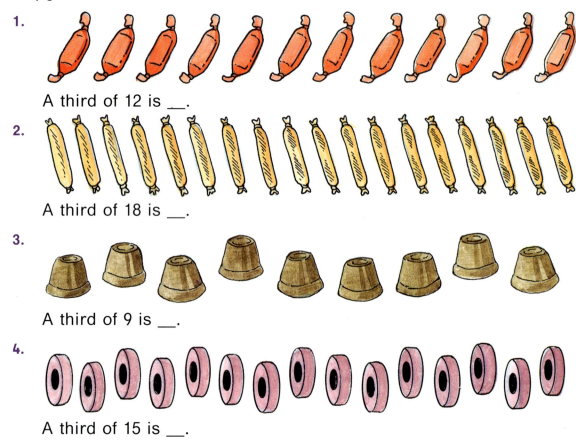

1. A third of 12 is __.

2. A third of 18 is __.

3. A third of 9 is __.

4. A third of 15 is __.

Division   Unit 3   Identifying a third of a set

Breaking up

> You will need small sticks or pieces of string and counters.

Use small sticks or pieces of string to cut these sets into equal parts. You could use counters to help you.

Copy and finish the sentences.

1. A half of __ is __.
2. A third of __ is __.

3. A half of __ is __.
4. A quarter of __ is __.

5. A half of __ is __.
6. A quarter of __ is __.
7. A third of __ is __.

8. A half of __ is __.
9. A third of __ is __.

Division   Unit 3   Identifying halves, thirds and quarters of sets

65

Number pictures

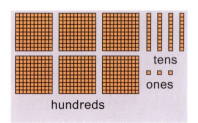

This number picture shows 643.

What do these pictures show?

1.
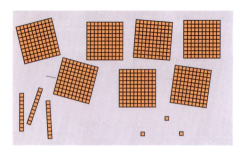

2.
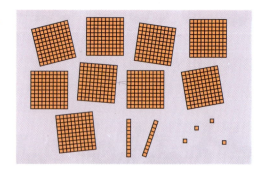

3.
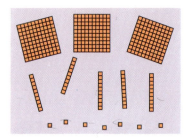

4.
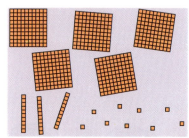

5.
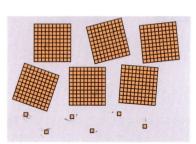

6.
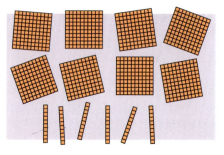

7.
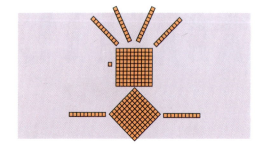

8.
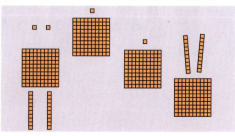

Numbers to 1000 Unit 4 *Translating from pictures to numerals*

Key numbers

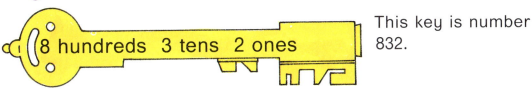

This key is number 832.

What numbers are these keys?

1.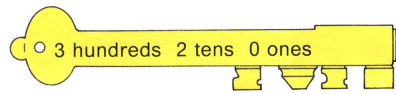

2.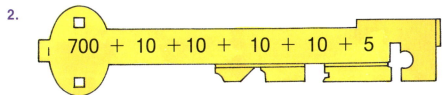

3.

4.

5.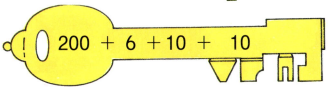

6.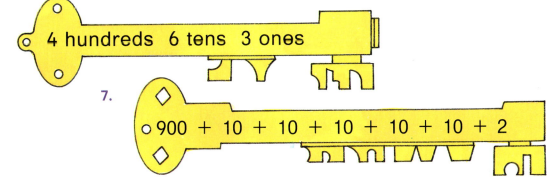

7.

Biggest and smallest

> Remember: > means "is bigger than"
> < means "is smaller than"

Using these cards

the biggest number I can make is

The smallest number I can make is

652 > 256

Make the biggest and smallest numbers with these cards. Write them using >.

1.  2.  3.

4.  5.  6.

Make the biggest and smallest numbers with these cards. Write them using <.

7.  8.  9.

10.  11.  12.

68 Numbers to 1000 Unit 5 Comparing 3-digit numbers using > and <

From smallest to biggest

| | 600 | 900 | 450 | 503 | 4 | 73 | 95 | 12 |

✏️➡️ 4   12   73   95   450   503   600   900

Write these numbers again, putting them in order, with the smallest number first and the biggest number last.

1. 427   93   862   112   68   75   603   222

2. 39   890   504   70   27   276   49   631

3. 104   103   987   61   550   702   130   201

4. 740   850   429   607   599   961   753   814

5. 999   3   86   115   311   95   270   166

6. 59   705   1   666   1000   340   383   141

Numbers to 1000   Unit 5   Ordering numbers to 1000

Pounds and purses

You will need real or pretend coins.

Write how much money is in each purse.

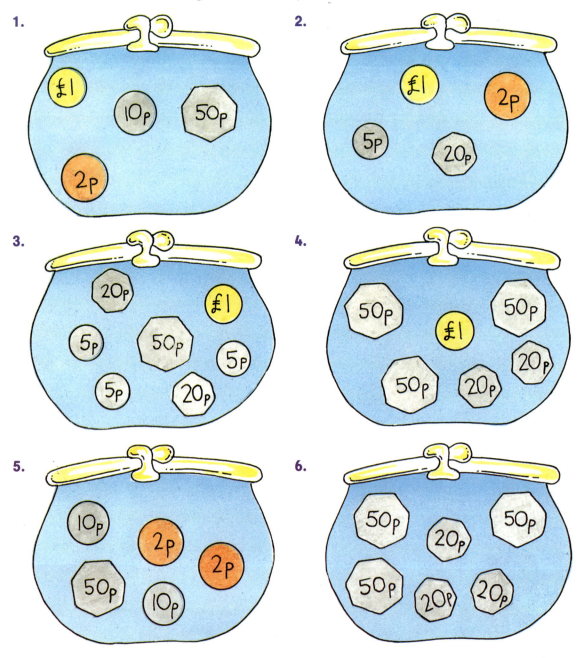

Small change

You will need real or pretend coins.

Sajida and Lucy each have £1.20.

Sajida has only two coins .

This is the smallest number of coins possible that make £1.20.

Draw the smallest number of coins possible to make these amounts.

1. £1.50
2. £0.78
3. £3.09

4. £2.94
5. £0.57
6. £4.66

Money *Unit 2* *Matching coins to amounts of money*

Can you add to these?

Copy the patterns. Write the missing numbers.

1. 36 = 30 + 6
    36 = 20 + 16
    36 = 10 + ☐

2. 54 = 50 + 4
    54 = 40 + 14
    54 = 30 + ☐
    54 = ☐ + ☐
    54 = ☐ + ☐

3. 39 = 30 + 9
    39 = ☐ + 19
    39 = ☐ + ☐

4. 62 = 60 + 2
    62 = ☐ + 12
    62 = ☐ + 22
    62 = ☐ + __
    62 = ☐ + __
    62 = ☐ + __

5. 71 = 70 + 1
    71 = 60 + 11
    71 = ☐ + ☐
    71 = ☐ + ☐
    71 = ☐ + ☐
    71 = ☐ + ☐
    71 = ☐ + ☐

6. 47 = 40 + 7
    47 = 30 + ☐
    47 = ☐ + ☐
    47 = ☐ + ☐

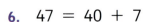

7. 124 = 100 + 20 + 4
    124 = 100 + 10 + 14
    124 = 100 + 0 + 24
    124 = 90 + 34
    124 = ☐ + ☐
    124 = ☐ + ☐

8. 137 = 100 + 30 + 7
    137 = ☐ + 20 + 17
    137 = 100 + ☐ + ☐
    137 = ☐ + 0 + ☐
    137 = ☐ + ☐
    137 = ☐ + ☐

Breaking up numbers

Can you break up numbers like this?
Make sure two of the parts are equal.

26 = 13 + 13 + 0
26 = 12 + 12 + 2
26 = 11 + 11 + 4
26 = 10 + 10 + 6

1. Continue the pattern. How far can you get?

Do the same with these numbers.

2. 20
3. 15
4. 11

How about three equal numbers?

22 = 7 + 7 + 7 + 1
22 = 6 + 6 + 6 + 4
22 = 5 + 5 + 5 + ?

5. Carry on as far as you can go.

Do the same with these numbers.

6. 17
7. 10
8. 15

Jason's model

Jason used these shapes to make his model.

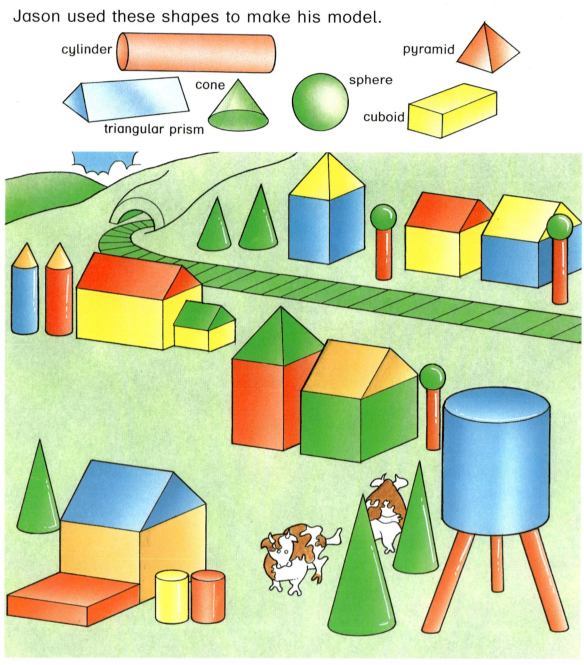

Look carefully at all the different shapes.
Answer the questions on the page.

3-D shapes   Unit 2   Identifying solid shapes in the environment

Questions

1. How many cones did he use?

2. What did he use pyramids for?

3. How many cuboids are there?

4. He used three cylinders for lamp-posts.
   How many more cylinders can you see?

5. Which shapes are the houses made of?

6. What did he use green cones for?

7. How many triangular prisms are there?

8. How many spheres did he use?

Now make your own model using solid shapes.

Write a list of all the shapes you use.
Then make up a quiz about your model to ask a friend.

Naming shapes

Shapes have different names. They are named after their number of sides.

triangles have 3 sides

quadrilaterals have 4 sides

pentagons have 5 sides

hexagons have 6 sides

heptagons have 7 sides

octagons have 8 sides

Name these shapes.

1. 2. 3. 4.

5. 6. 7. 8.

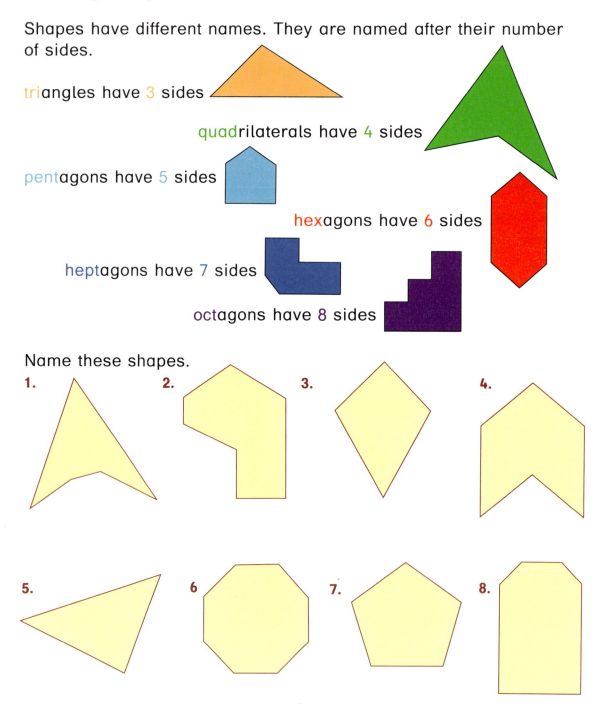

Use a ruler to draw your own shapes.
Count the sides and name your shapes.

Tile patterns

This triangle was cut out and
drawn around to make this tile pattern.

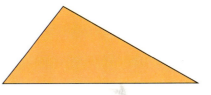

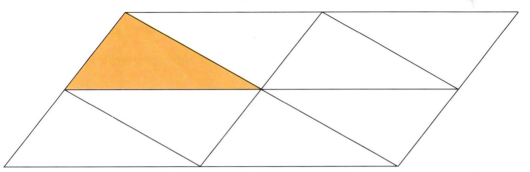

Triangles fit together well.
They tessellate.

Trace these shapes onto card. Cut them out.
Draw around each one to see if they tessellate.

1.
2.
3.
4.

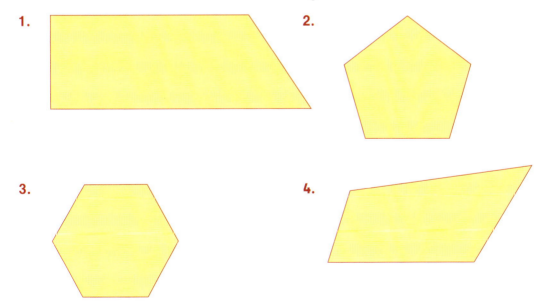

Draw your own unusual shape.
Try to use it to make a tessellating pattern.

How long?

Estimate how long these are.

Measure and write down the answers.

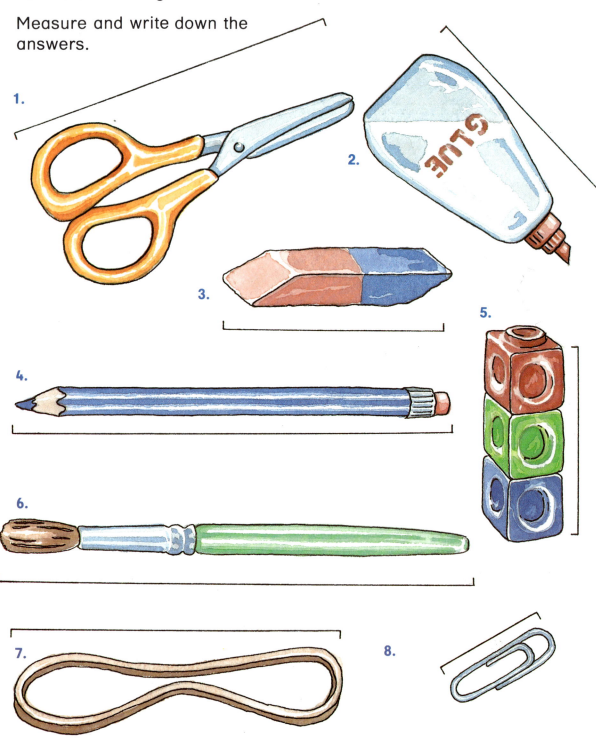

Measure these paths

Measure each line.
Add up the measurements.
Find the longest path.

2 cm + 1 cm + 3 cm = 6 cm

1.

2.

3.
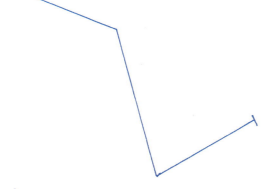

4.
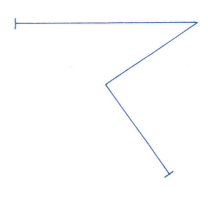

5.
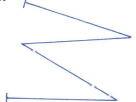

Use your ruler to measure and draw these paths.

6. 6 cm + 1 cm = 7 cm

7. 7 cm + 9 cm = 16 cm

8. 8 cm + 3 cm + 2 cm = 13 cm

9. 4 cm + 5 cm + 3 cm = 12 cm

10. 6 cm + 3 cm + 4 cm = 13 cm

Length   Unit 3   Measuring and drawing lines

Making timers

You need:
yoghurt pots
a tray or large container
dry sand or water
something to make a small hole with
a timer.

How to do it:

Make a very small hole in the bottom of the yoghurt pot.

Keep your finger over the hole.
Fill the pot with water or dry sand.

Put a tray or large container underneath to catch the water or sand.

Now start the timer and take your finger away from the hole.
A friend could help you with this.

Time how long it takes the water or sand to run out.

Some tests to try:

1. Test your timer three times. Does it always take the same time to run out?

2. Make the hole a little bigger and do the tests again. What difference does it make?

3. Try to make a timer that always takes about three minutes to run out.

4. Can you make a timer which could be used to time playtime?

A race against time

Some friends had a race.
These were the times on the stop-watches.

Jo took 32 seconds.

1. Write down the times for each of the others.
2. Put their times in order, from shortest to longest.
3. Who came first?
4. Who came third?
5. Who came last?
6. What is the difference between the shortest time and the longest?
7. How long did Jo have to wait for Anita to finish?
8. Who was quickest, Paul or Anita?

Make a square

> You will need newspaper, scissors, sellotape and a metre stick.

Measure with the metre stick.

Make a square of newspaper 1 metre long and 1 metre wide.

The newspaper has an area of one square metre.

Compare it with these areas. Copy and complete the table.

	Smaller than one square metre	About one square metre	Greater than one square metre
Your table top			
A window sill			
A window			
A door			

Choose some other things to measure.
For example, a blackboard, a radiator, a shelf.

You can fold your paper to help you check carefully.

Area   Unit 1   Comparing areas to one square metre

Measuring flowers

> You will need scissors and card.

 Cut a square exactly this size from card.

On this plan of a flower bed your square represents one square metre. Use it to measure.

1. What area is covered by red flowers?
2. What area is covered by yellow flowers?
3. What area is covered by orange flowers?
4. What area is covered by blue flowers?
5. What area is covered by purple flowers?
6. What area is covered by pink flowers?

Favourite flavours

Tina wanted to find out how many ice-creams she had sold.

She needed to order some more.

She also wanted to find out which flavour was the most popular.

She drew this pictogram to show the information.

Title ⟶

Ice-cream Cones Sold	
Vanilla	🍦🍦
Chocolate	🍦🍦🍦🍦
Strawberry	🍦
Neapolitan	🍦
Coffee	🍦🍦🍦
Choc-mint chip	🍦🍦🍦
🍦 means 4 cones	

Key ⟶

Remember, each picture means 4 ice-creams.

Half a picture means half of 4, which is 2.

How many of these did she sell?

1. Vanilla
2. Coffee
3. Choc Mint Chip
4. Neapolitan
5. Which flavour is the most popular?
6. Which flavour is the hardest to sell?

How many ice-creams would these pictures show?

7.

8.

9.

Exploring pictograms

How many children come to school this way?

1. cycling

2. by bus

3. by car

4. walking

5. How many more children walk than cycle?

6. How many children do not walk to school?

Now make your own pictogram.

Find out how the children in your class come to school.

Choose a picture you like for the Key.

Draw your pictogram.

Don't forget to put a title on your pictogram.

Glossary

bar chart
A graph where bars stand for numbers or measurements.

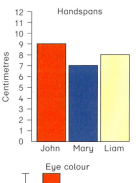

block graph
A graph where columns are in blocks. Each block stands for one thing.

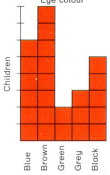

centimetre (cm)   A measure of length.

circle

cone

cube   A special cuboid with all its faces square (see cuboid).

cuboid   A 3-D shape with 6 faces. All the faces are rectangles. All the corners are right-angles. Sometimes called a rectangular prism.

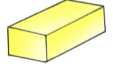

cylinder

estimate   What you think an answer might be.

half When you share things equally between two, each share is a half. When you cut a shape into two equal pieces, each piece is a half.

hexagon Any shape with 6 straight sides.

hour (hr) A measure of time. The time it takes for the big hand of a clock to go all the way round. There are 60 minutes in an hour.

kilogram (kg) A measure of weight.

litre (l) A measure of how much a container holds (capacity).

metre (m) A measure of length. 1 m = 100 cm

minute (min) A measure of time. The time it takes for the second hand of a watch to go all the way round. There are 60 seconds in a minute.

octagon Any shape with 8 straight sides.

pentagon Any shape with 5 straight sides.

pictogram A graph where pictures stand for things.

predict To work out what will happen or what the result will be.

prism A solid that is the same shape all the way through.

triangular prism

rectangular prism

pyramid

rectangular pyramid

triangular pyramid

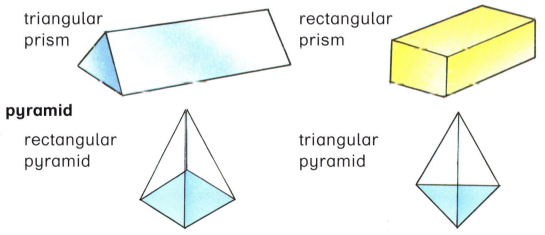

Glossary

quadrilateral Any shape with four straight sides.

quarter When you share things equally between four, each share is a quarter. When you cut a shape into 4 equal pieces, each piece is a quarter.

rectangle A 2-D shape with 4 straight sides; all the angles are right angles.

right-angle Like the corner of this page.

second (sec) A measure of time.

semi-circle Half a circle.

sphere A ball shape.

square A special rectangle with all the sides equal (see rectangle).

square metre (m²) A square with sides that are 1 metre long. A measure of area.

tessellate To fit shapes together without gaps.

third When you share equally between three, each share is a third. When you cut a shape into 3 equal pieces, each piece is a third.

triangle Any shape with 3 straight sides.

< is less than. 3 < 6 means 3 is less than 6.

> is greater than. 6 > 3 means 6 is greater than 3.